a diary
MEANS YES
indeed.
~ GERTRUDE STEIN

Art Doodle Love

A Journal of Self-Discovery

Dawn DeVries Sokol

STC Craft | A Melanie Falick Book

stewart tabori & chang
An imprint of ABRAMS

Published in 2013 by Stewart, Tabori & Chang
An imprint of ABRAMS

Library of Congress Cataloging-in-Publication Data

Sokol, Dawn DeVries.
Art doodle love / by Dawn DeVries Sokol.
pages cm
ISBN 978-1-61769-012-9 (alk. paper)
1. Handicraft. 2. Doodles. I. Title.

TT157.S59 2013
745.5—dc23

2012022907

Editor: Liana Allday
Designer: Dawn DeVries Sokol
Production Manager: Tina Cameron

The text of this book was composed in Marydale.

Printed and bound in the United States
10

Stewart, Tabori & Chang books are available at special discounts when purchased in quantity for premiums
and promotions as well as fundraising or educational use. Special editions can also be created to specifica-
tion. For details, contact specialsales@abramsbooks.com or the address below.

THE ART OF BOOKS SINCE 1949

115 West 18th Street
New York, NY 10011
www.abramsbooks.com

Contents

INTRODUCTION:
why did You

Welcome to ART DOODLE LOVE, a guided journal of self-discovery and artful acceptance. Short of inviting you on a global adventure to find yourself — like Elizabeth Gilbert's journey in the memoir EAT PRAY LOVE — I conjured ART DOODLE LOVE to help you go on an emotional journey and find your inner artist.

But first, why did you pick up this book? Do you incessantly doodle in meetings, classes, or on the train to work? Maybe, like I once did, you're a little bored with the written form of expression, so you scribble in the margins of your journal alongside the words? Basically, if you have any desire at all to use art AND words to express your thoughts, then you are well on your way to keeping what is called an "art journal."

Art journaling is an artistic avenue for creating, visualizing, and documenting your life. While writing in a journal is a valuable tool, some people feel limited using just words. Plus, many of us underestimate the importance of visualization and how it maps out our thoughts and ideas. When you use color, collage, doodles, and paints to express yourself, it opens up a whole new way of experiencing and interpreting the world via the right side of your brain.

Even if you don't journal daily, the benefits of keeping a journal are endless. We discover ourselves through our journals — our loves, desires,

pick up this book?

needs, hopes, and fears. A journal documents our lives in a way no other record does. It offers a place to spill and dump all the nitty-gritty and daily tidbits that we may otherwise lose or forget in this age of information overload. We also need a place to leave all those brilliant little sparks of ideas that could one day mature into something big. Often, I backtrack through my journals for ideas when I'm feeling creatively drained. This process energizes and renews me, and also squashes the feelings of doubt about my creative ability that may seep in when I'm spiraling into an artistic rut.

You may be thinking, "Art journaling sounds awesome, but how and where do I start? How do I get past that blank page?"

There are many steps to creating a layered, mixed-media art journal page, but these techniques can be overwhelming to someone just starting out, inhibiting many beginners. In this book, I've provided prompts and painted pages to give you a jump start into art journaling so you won't have to figure out the major techniques before diving in. The ideas and backgrounds will be there for you, guiding you into that creative zone, and these pretty pages become even lovelier when you doodle and draw all over them, adding bits of ephemera to your heart's content.

BUT FIRST, A BIT ABOUT ME

Always a crafty girl, I never considered myself artistic. My teachers told me early on that I was a writer and not a natural artist. I was too young to realize it at the time, but I had been labeled. My brother, who had a "natural talent," was encouraged to draw and paint as much as he desired. I would accompany my mother to pick him up from the local city art center and loved every bit of the studio: the smell of paint, the way the light streamed in through the lofty windows, the creative vibe. At home, my mother guided me in all the crafty goodness of the time, like knitting, macramé, and embroidery, but I was jealous of my brother's paints and pastels and his ability to draw scenery.

So I avoided trying. I proclaimed for most of my life that I couldn't draw a straight line or even a stick figure. I attended journalism school and started working at the copy desk at my local newspaper. While at the newspaper, I started designing pages and then special sections. This was a time in the newspaper industry when the design process was going digital, and I taught myself the necessary programs to design pages. Soon enough I wanted more visual creativity in my job and found myself art directing magazines and designing books. I felt like a designer but still believed art was out of my reach. It wasn't until 2000, when I walked into a paper arts store, that I suddenly felt I had arrived home. I took every workshop they offered — from rubber-stamping to beading — and bought mountains of books teaching mixed-media techniques.

In 2003, after learning about ARTFEST, an alternative arts retreat held in Port Townsend, Washington, I found a friend who was willing to make the trek with me, and off we went. What I didn't foresee was how much I would be emotionally awakened on that excursion, from realizing that I was still mourning the sudden death of my father a couple of years earlier, to learning how to take the artist within myself seriously. At this retreat, I learned that everyone is an artist. Whether we admit it or not, creativity resides within all of us, and our hunger to bring it to the surface is what allows it to flourish. The entire trip was an emotional journey that left me longing for an artistic life.

After attending ARTFEST and other retreats, I started to realize that "art" goes beyond the ability to draw realistically — art is creation of any kind with any material the artist wishes. I challenged myself with many mediums, making precious-metal clay charms, beading, rubber-stamping, and working with fibers and collage. When I discovered the art of "art journaling," I have to admit I didn't quite understand the appeal. Why would you want to paint, collage, write, and spill your creative thoughts into a book, then close the covers and put it away where no one can see it? At that point, I still had it in my head that art was about display. But with time I came to discover that art is really about self-expression — whether anyone sees it or not — and art journaling is one of the truest forms of documenting our deepest desires, our dreams, our thoughts, and our craziest ideas. In fact, because it's so private, the art journal is an ideal place for an artist to be herself.

Maintaining an art journal transformed me, offering a safe place to explore techniques, play with composition, and express myself with words, colors, and images.

HOW TO USE THIS BOOK

No matter where you are on your path to embracing an artist's mindset, you can still rock this book! I've geared it toward those looking for an art journaling/doodling jump start, a way to get past all the technicalities and just JOURNAL.

Once you learn what supplies you'll need (page 14), we'll move on to "Finding the Mojo" (page 22), where I will throw out some exercises to get you energized and your doodle juices flowing. Then we can really start exploring! In the next chapter, "My Life Then" (page 40), I'll help you take a look at your past self, all through doodling, collage, and writing. In chapter three, "My Life Now" (page 68), we'll do the same exploration but on the present you. The next chapter, "Wanderlust" (page 102), provides a way for you to escape your daily life by doodling your journeys, no matter how near or far. In the final chapter, "Love, Like, and Hate" (page 132), I'll help you doodle your way through your relationships.

Of course, as you embark on this doodling journey, I want you to follow a few simple guidelines:

1. Interpret the prompts in whatever way feels comfortable to you (i.e., the results can be simple or more complicated, silly or serious, and may take you down a different road entirely from the one you intended).
2. It's okay if you spend more time on some prompts than others.
3. Feel free to skip around in the book. Find a page that feels right for you at the time and start doodling.
4. You are not required to finish a page all in one sitting.
5. There are NO rules in this book, meaning anything you do within these covers is appropriate and is totally up to you. In other words, free your mind and the doodle will follow!

Finally, my annoying inner cheerleader has a few more words to say. (I know it's a little peppy, but bear with me...don't skip ahead! We all need a pep talk once in a while, even if we don't know it.)

SO many budding artists claim they can't draw and shudder at the thought of "learning how" to be creative. Yeah, I was that woman, too. Been there, done that. Now let's end this pity party.

WE'RE ALL CREATIVE. We just need to open our minds to possibility. "No" isn't in our vocabulary anymore, at least not when referring to art. We eat, we breathe, we sleep, we create. Period. Hate your handwriting? Get over it. Hate the way you doodle? Chill! It's not the end of the world. Stop comparing your art to others', stop believing you can't draw, can't doodle, can't write, blah, blah, blah.

It's not rocket science. It's not life or death. It's art journaling — pure and simple. Take all your worries and self-criticisms and chuck them out the window. Your art journal is your safe place — easy to close up and hide away if you need to, and just as easy to open up and explore when you're ready. That's the beauty of this creative format.

ALSO: There's no "learning how" to doodle. We all know how. You'll see quickie tips throughout the book to guide you along, but trust your inner doodler. She's in there.

You CAN create. You CAN keep an art journal. In ART DOODLE LOVE, you don't have to worry about "ruining" anything by making marks on these pages. From now on, your hand is golden, your artistic voice is clear. Dump those insecurities altogether.

You can be girly, you can be flowery — you can be powerful, strong, juicy, and vibrant. You can be whoever you want to be today.

You ARE art!

SUPPLIES:
the art journaling arsenal

The quintessential tool for art journaling is, of course, a pen. Yet some are preferable to others. A ballpoint pen alone would do the trick for this book, but if you want to gather some other types of pens, I've made suggestions in this section. Most of these tools are sold individually, which is great if you just want to test them out. You can always buy whole sets with more colors or variations later.

black felt-tip pens

MICRON 05

I gravitate toward Sakura Micron pens or Faber-Castell PITT pens for writing and doodling. Both are waterproof and fade-proof, but the Micron tips vary more in size. If you like to doodle with thicker lines, try tips ranging from .05 and higher. If you like skinnier lines, try tips .03, .01, and lower.

gel pens

My favorite gel pens are from Sakura, and I prefer the Soufflé and Glaze pens. Glaze pens dry with a jewel-like translucency, whereas the pastel Soufflés dry as a raised, opaque layer of goodness.

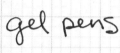

GELLY ROLL *Glaze*

white pens

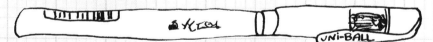

UNI-BALL

The uni-ball Signo UM-153 is a Japanese white pen that writes easily over painted surfaces. I usually buy mine at JetPens.com, but this pen is becoming more readily available in U.S. scrapbooking stores. A white correction fluid pen or a white Soufflé pen are possible substitutes for the UM-153, but they won't flow as well.

markers

I love to use Tombow Dual Brush Pens; they have a different tip at each end and come in a wide variety of colors.

If you're just starting out, I recommend getting a set of good old-fashioned Crayola Washable Markers. They are less pricey and readily available in most office supply stores and big-box stores, and their color quality is comparable to the Tombows.

pencils

The ol' No. 2 will suffice, but if you want to be fancy, grab any HB pencil.

I've found that using an eraser keeps people from being more accepting of or open-minded about their doodles, so I hope if you do use a pencil, you won't succumb to the eraser.

colored pencils/watercolor pencils

Any brand on the market will do, but to get more bang for your buck, try Derwent Inktense Pencils, which work as both colored pencils and watercolor pencils. When the pencils are wet, the colors pop off the page.

adhesives

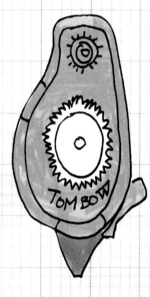

When attaching collage bits, Tombow's Mono Adhesive roller is my go-to. The glue is applied to the surface through a tape roller, so there's no mess, and the adhesive holds extremely well.

GLUESTICK Glue sticks will also work fine, but I prefer the Tombow Mono.

The best thing about both glue sticks and the Tombow Mono is they won't seep out from under collage bits like regular glue, which keeps pages from sticking together.

Instead of adhesives, you can use paper clips, stickers, photo corners, brads, staples, pretty paper tapes (called Washi tapes), or even Scotch tape.

ephemera

Don't be afraid to collect bits from your everyday life to paste onto the pages. You'll be amazed at how they transform your pages and tell your story. Hold on to candy wrappers, receipts, labels, fruit stickers — anything that twirls your skirt. I've even held on to the "grass" from sushi trays (as shown on pages 44–45)! And for a truly personal touch, make color photocopies of old family photos to use in collages, even if they are black and white, since color copies retain the quality and tint of the original.

Scissors

Of course, the arsenal wouldn't be complete without a pair of scissors. I prefer to use Honey Bee scissors by EK Success, which you can find at craft stores. They're small, so they are easy to transport, and the smaller tips allow you to make very fine cuts and get into hard-to-reach places. They also have a nonstick surface, so you can cut sticky items without having to worry about adhesive residue.

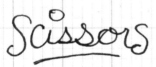

portable printer

Having a portable printer on hand makes it so easy to art journal on the fly. Depending on what type of camera you have, you can print photos directly to the Polaroid PoGo! The PoGo prints 2 x 3 inch images on photo paper with a sticky back, so you can simply peel the backing off the photo and stick it where you please.

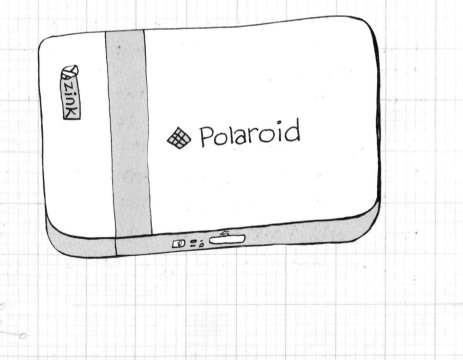

intention

PAGE

I would like to find out stuff about myself that I may not realize yet. Although I think this book is very interesting I'm not sure how its going to help me develope a better relationship with myself. I'm good at art but I'm not good at doodling even handed so I'm hoping that this book can help me out. I'm not great at journalling because I never really know what to write down. Overall, I really hope to find more out about myself. I want to realize and figure certain things out that I may not have been able to if it weren't for art. I would like to learn as much as possible but I'm not really sure how I can do that. Hopefully I'm wrong and I will think of art differently because it may really help me out. I'm hoping

20

that I can get through certain situations with the help of this journal. I'm really hoping to get really good at making cool art and doodles. I would like to become a more artsy person. I wouldn't mind developing self-confidence and bringing my self-esteem and body image up. I would enjoy learning things about anything that I probably didn't know. Learning how to understand others in the best way possible would be nice. I would like art and doodling to help me become a better person. I want to become a more creative person or just find my creativity.

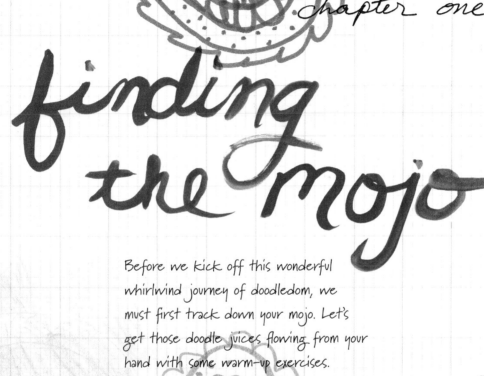

23

chapter one

finding the mojo

Before we kick off this wonderful whirlwind journey of doodledom, we must first track down your mojo. Let's get those doodle juices flowing from your hand with some warm-up exercises.

Scribble

anything on this page

What do you see within these ink splotches and drips?
Doodle from them and around them.

26

flower power

Doodle from the spots of color to turn them into flowers.
Fill the whole page with your doodles.

Fill the colored areas with a
doodle of ANYTHING each
day for a week.

a doodle a day

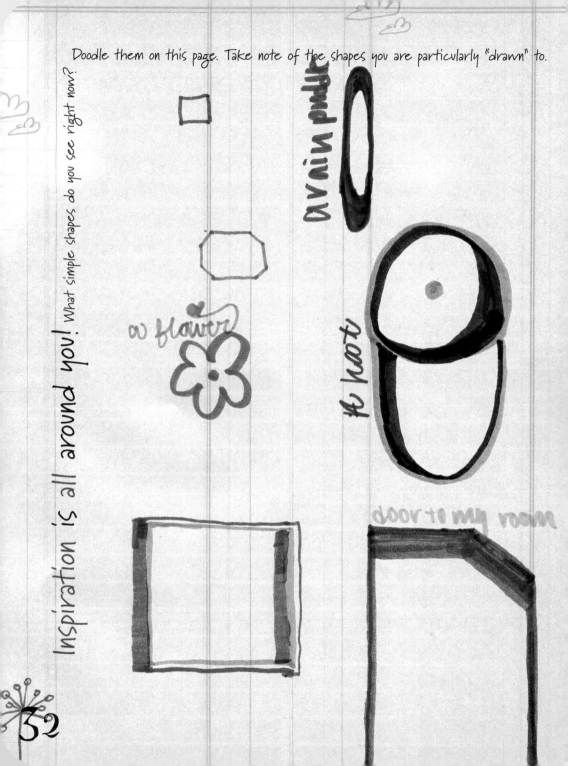

Doodle them on this page. Take note of the shapes you are particularly "drawn" to.

Inspiration is all around you! What simple shapes do you see right now?

a vain pull

a hoot

a flower

door to my room

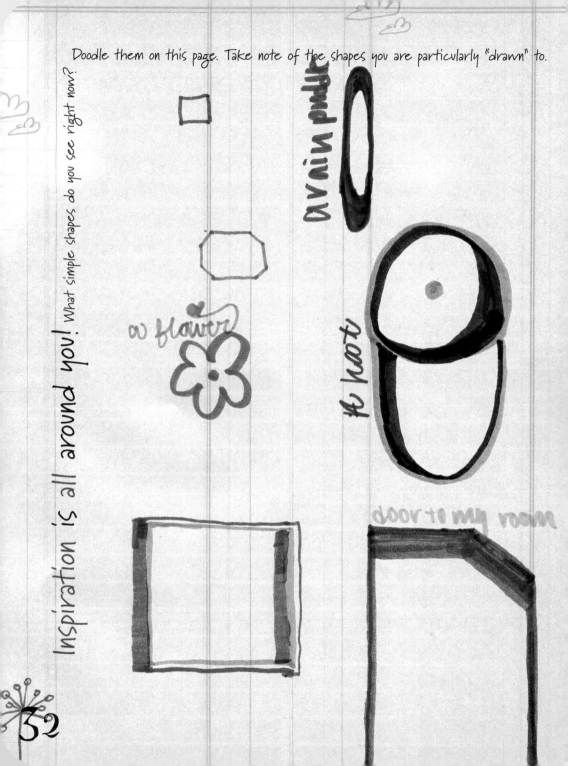

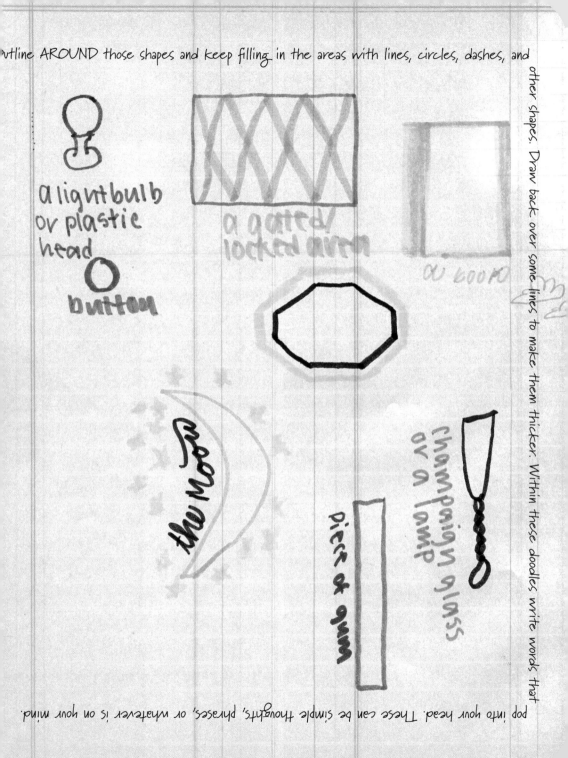

a lightbulb
or plastic
head

a gated/
locked arm

button

the moon

a door

champaign glass
or a lamp

piece of gum

other shapes. Draw back over some lines to make them thicker. Within these doodles write words that

34

garden party

Try going to a garden, park, or arboretum and doodling the shapes you see. Most plants and flowers are easy to draw if you think of them as simple shapes combined in different ways. For example, a daisy is a circle with skinny ovals doodled out from the center.

go with the

Try doodling without thinking too much about it. Start
your doodles using the background swirls as a guide and
keep going from there!

flow

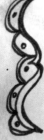

Stuck on black felt-tip pens? Try using a new pen today. Or use your black pen in combination with a white gel pen to add more depth.

Monotone

Create a collage out of everyday materials, like receipts, candy wrappers, or anything imaginable. Try to use only shades of a single color.

39

chapter two

my life then

In this section, we'll be exploring who you were in the past: your feelings, your childhood, and how you viewed yourself. Some pages are for everyday explorations, and others encourage you to go deeper. If certain prompts speak to you, repeat them to fill other pages that are promptless. (And don't forget to date your entries!)

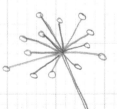

let go of...

expectations:

Collage, doodle, and write anything from the past you wish to release. After that, cover the entire page with positive thoughts and images. By documenting the issues that have always bothered you, you can start to put them behind you.

worries:

stresses:

One word to describe my childhood home:

my Childhood
home

[If you have a picture of your home, paste it here. If not, try to doodle how you remember it.]

My memories of living there:

Doodle the floorplan of your childhood home and describe it.

You can also doodle features or aspects of the house or its surroundings.

My bedroom was:

My siblings were:

My parents were:

Best/worst moments in that home:

then...

Paste a photo of yourself from when you were younger on this page. Journal, collage, and doodle around it. Who were you then? What were your likes and interests?

What has happened in your life that you'll want to remember forever? Take note on these pages using words, doodles, and collage.

things to

remember

Songs I loved in high school:

Songs I will love my whole life:

Songs from my childhood:

When I hear the song _____,
it makes me think of:

my life's soundtrack

oh, happy day!

Doodle/collage/write about a moment in
time you can call your happiest yet.

laughing-stock

Write about a moment in the past that made you laugh. Make sure to note who you were with, where, when, and why.

6θ

fold of fabri

ligne sur la pliur du t

la linea sobre el doblez

19

62

time

Paste a photo of yourself from ten or more years ago on this page, then draw how you saw yourself next to it. Don't worry, it doesn't have to be "realistic."

Focus on just your face, if you want, or maybe just a feature of your face...whatever you feel comfortable with.

fear not

We all have fears. Some are stronger than others, and some are more rational than others. List and doodle your former fears and how you conquered them.

chapter three

my life now

Now that you've examined your past, let's take a look at the present. In this chapter, you'll go on a soul search through your day-to-day life. What are you learning? What do you notice? Make sure to date your entries!

Soul Search

Discovering what feeds the soul is vital to happiness.
So, it's time to wander...

What parts of your life feed your soul?

What are your hopes and dreams?
Remember, NOTHING is out of reach.

Find a quote about dreams and write/
doodle/collage it here.

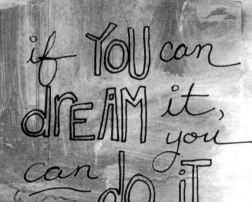

if YOU can dream it, you can do it.

~WALT DISNEY

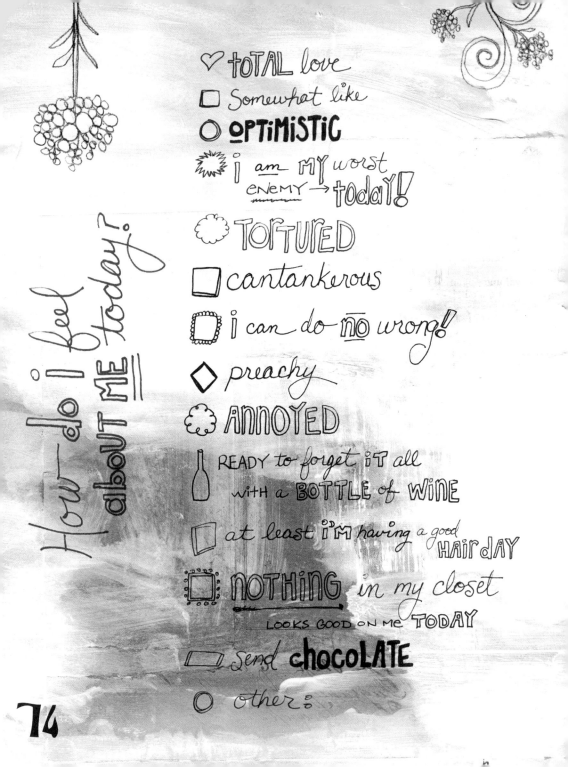

♡ tOTAL love

□ somewhat like

O OPTiMiSTiC

☼ i am MY worst enemy → today!

☁ TORTURED

□ cantankerous

▢ i can do no wrong!

◇ preachy

❀ ANNOYED

🍾 READY to forget it all with a BOTTLE of WINE

□ at least i'M having a good HAiR DAY

▣ NOTHiNG in my closet LOOKS GOOD ON ME TODAY

▭ send chocoLATE

O other:

How do i feel about ME today?

74

Doodle and/or collage any other emotions you may feel about yourself today.

in my head

5 random words that pop into your head:

How do these words make you feel?

5 things that happened today:

How do these things make you feel?

...and now

Paste a current photo of yourself on this page and journal/doodle around it. Who are you now? What are your likes and interests?

beLIEVE in:

UNDERSTAND:

aspire to:

today i:

dReAM of:

HOPE for:

81

Try not to ponder
your answers too long,
and add doodles next to
your words, if possible.

lust for:

PREDICT:

ENVISION:

pursue:

Say Me

Find a quote (or quotes) that personifies you.

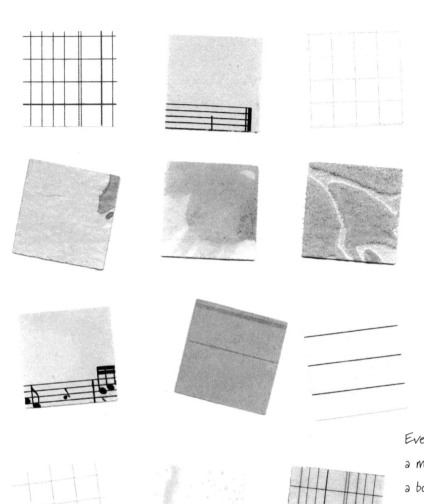

Every day for
a month, fill in
a box with a doodle
or thought about one
thing for which you
are grateful.

Use a pen that will show up well on this background, like a Soufflé pen or a uni-ball Signo UM-153 pen.

When we are
UNABLE to FIND
tranquility within ourselves,
IT IS USELESS to seek it elsewhere.

— FRANÇOIS DE LA
ROCHEFOUCAULD

1:

2≈

5 things that
make me smile

time for

Whether it's a life-altering event or a more subtle change, what is it time for you to do in your life?

today i.

learned

95

why can't i?

What holds you back? Let your mind go and doodle/spill all that is keeping you from fulfilling your dreams.

my coat of colors

On one page, doodle and use colors you think personify you. On the facing page, doodle and use colors you WISH personified you.

Think of shapes that personify you while you're doodling.

98

What values can you live by that will make you a better person? List and doodle them here.

my affirmations

NOTHING
CAN BRING YOU
peace BUT
YOURSELF.
^RALPH WALDO EMERSON

SOMETIMES

you HAVE to GO away
to DISCOVER

where you've been.

~ UNKNOWN

chapter four

Wanderlust

Whether we travel to distant lands or simply explore our own surroundings, where and how we roam speaks volumes about who we are. Within this chapter, we will discover ourselves through the journeys we take.

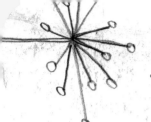

from where

Wherever you are, look around, breathe in, and take note.

Doodle what you see, or take a photo and paste it on the page. Look around with a "wide-angle lens" or focus your eyes on the details.

i sit

i smell:

i see:

i TASTE:

i HEAR:

i feel:

How do your surroundings affect your outlook?

What is the color palette of your surroundings?

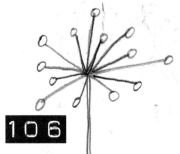

How does this color palette make you feel?

Your WORK is to
DISCOVER YOUR
WORLD AND THEN WITH
all your ♡ give
YOURSELF to
it.

~BUDDHA

108

day mapping

Where did you go today?
Map it out on these pages.

How do you feel after this day?

What parts of it affected you the most?

What were the highlights?

What were the lowlights?

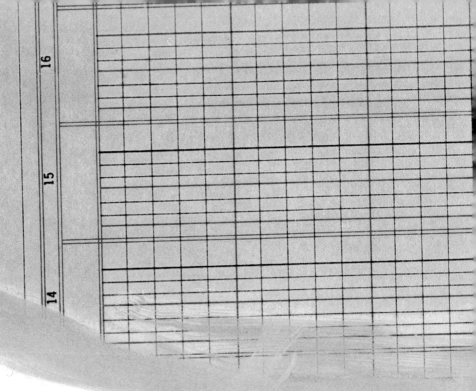

Where do you want to be?
Where do you feel your best?

finding my best me

11⁶

Paste a photo of yourself on this page and doodle around it to create a scene of where you'd like to be.

Whether it's the back patio, a restaurant, or an imaginary setting, where do you go when you need to make the mess disappear?

my

happy place

a week of faces

Doodle a face in each of the boxes over the course of one week. They can be the expressions on your own face this week, or the faces of people you encounter.

my dream hometown

Where in the world would you want to put down roots?

BY AIR MAIL

航 PAR AVION 空

A

Royal Mail

POSTAGE PAID   UK

£5.60   KY13

1.31402641

i TASTE:

i see:

i feel:

the five

i smell ö

i HEAr:

senses

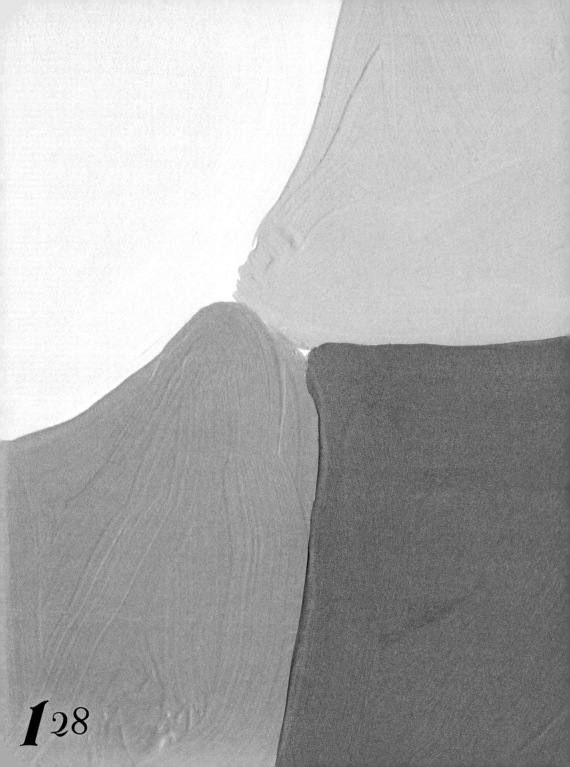

a week of
daily doodles

For one week,
fill each space on
these pages with
doodles of what
happened each day.

IT is the journey, NOT the destination.
it is the story, NOT the ENDING.

~ UNKNOWN

chapter five

like, and hate

Your relationships with those around you
influence your life, whether you like
it or not. Let's explore those ties and how
they relate to you and your creativity.

Paste a photo of a person who is important to you on this page.
How have they affected you?

☐ *am a loner*

☐ AM able to hang out by myself, BUT _love_ MY friends, too.

☐ *need* PEOPLE AROUND me always!

If you love to be around others, take yourself out to lunch or a movie. If you are a loner, attend a party or an event with a crowd. If you're in between, try both experiences and compare. Write, doodle, and collage how this made you feel.

my life's

garden

Imagine that you live in a garden surrounded by all kinds of plants and flowers — these are the people in your life. What kinds of plants and flowers do you see? Doodle, collage, and describe them on these pages.

1^{40}

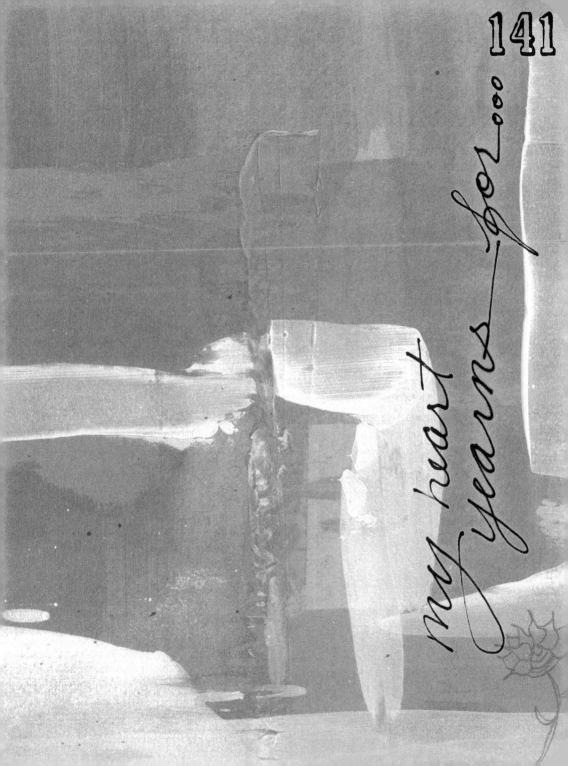

my heart
yearns for...

cleaning

Once in a while, we need to clean out the bad energy in our lives, and sometimes that means people. Anyone in your life exuding negativity? Find a photo of the person (or something that represents them) and paste it here. Now collage over the rest of the page with pretty papers and images, and doodle happy symbols and feelings.

*1*46

*those i
have loved*

who — makes me happy?

Surround yourself
with these people.
They're for keeps!

DON't forget
to love YOURSELf.

~SØREN KIERKEGAARD

List things you've learned about yourself from this journal.

How have you changed since your first doodle in this book?

creative

So what's next?

goals

{ love and thanks

TJ ~ FOR MAKING MY
LIFE SO MUCH
MORE

— RON,
FOR BEING
SUCH a
GREAT BROTHER

DOTTI
MY CHEERLEADER

← MOM —
FOR
[BELIEVING]
IN ME

LUCY —
MY FAITHFUL
CONFIDANTE &
STUDIO BUDDY

JEAN
SAGENDORPH
POCKER,
MY RELENTLESS
LITERARY

MICHELLE WITHE-
ADAMS ~
JENNIFER
for that link
FOR THE FIRST COUPLE OF BOOKS THAT
LED ME HERE

1963 mow hu

1 58

LiANA allday, EDITOR EXTRAORDINAIRE · Melanie FALICK, PUBLISHER EXTRAORDINAIRE · the awesome TEAM @ABRAMS/STC CRAFT

MY BLOG READERS AND STUDENTS, for the way THEY INSPIRE ME

teesha and tracy MOORE FOR PROVIDING ME WITH A PLACE to BLOOM

MICHAEL DERR, for encouraging me YEARS AGO to DO WHAT I WANTED to do

and DAD, WHO taught ME PATIENCE AND optimism, EVEN after HE LEFT tHIS EARTH. i♥U!

2012 &

about the author

Dawn DeVries Sokol doodles in her art journals as much as she can when she's not teaching at live retreats and on her blog at dawndsokol.com. Her studio is a mess of papers, pens, paints, inks, and books she loves, and her dog Lucy is always nearby, patiently waiting for their next walk. Sokol has authored and designed several books, including 1000 ARTIST JOURNAL PAGES, DOODLE DIARY, and DOODLE SKETCHBOOK, and she recently decorated a utility box and library card with her doodles for the City of Tempe in Arizona. Her art journals have been exhibited in galleries from Phoenix, Arizona, to Tokyo, Japan. She hopes to someday color all of the world with her doodles.